Be Grateful

Eileen Teel

Fulton Books
Meadville, PA

Published by Fulton Books 2024

ISBN 979-8-88982-568-5 (paperback)
ISBN 979-8-88982-569-2 (digital)

Printed in the United States of America

For baby Harold Brian McGinnis

Grace and Patrick were excited for the weekend. This weekend, they get to have a sleepover at Grandma and Papa's house.

As their mom was busily packing their clothes, books, toothbrushes, and favorite blankets, she reminded them that they had three days and two nights to enjoy with their grandparents.

"You are so lucky that your grandparents live so close to us. And Daddy and I are grateful, too! We get some time alone to be with one another."

"Wow," said Grace, "I can't wait!"

"Me too!" Patrick said.

The children were so excited, they both went into the playroom and talked about what fun things they were looking forward to.

"I bet we get to go to the green park!" Grace screamed out with excitement.

"Yeah, and I'm going to climb the big tower," said Patrick.

"Okay, children," Mom said. "Are you ready to go?" She continued, "I'll help you into your car seats. Everyone ready?"

"We are ready," said Patrick. "Let's go!"

As Mom turned down the street to Grandma and Papa's house, Patrick yelled, "We are almost there!"

"Yeah, I can see their house!" said Grace.

Papa and Grandma were standing at the front door. They were just as excited as the children!

"Hello there!" Papa said with much excitement.

"Grandma!" Grace said while jumping up to give her grandma a big hug.

Grace waved as Mom drove off. "Bye, Mom, love you!"

The first thing the children did was run into their bedroom. They had had so many sleepovers, they knew exactly where to go.

Grace took out her flowered blanket first.

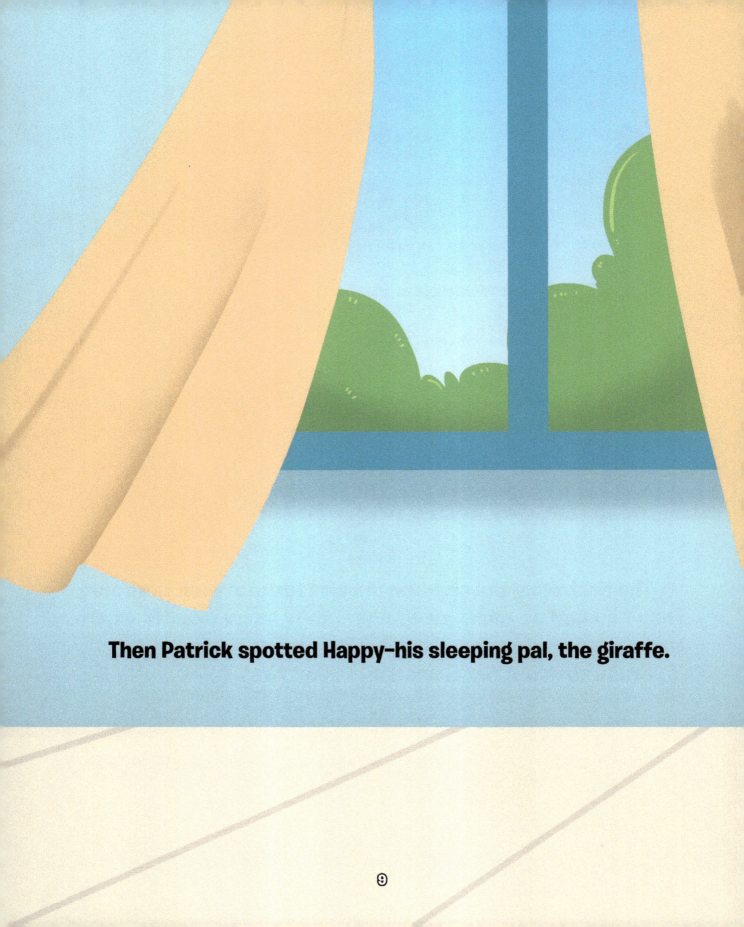

Then Patrick spotted Happy–his sleeping pal, the giraffe.

The children put away everything that Mom packed for them. They thought about what their mom said about being grateful. Patrick smiled and said to Grace, "I am grateful to be here with Grandma and Papa."

After coloring and putting together some crafts, it was time for bed.

Papa read the children a book and tucked them in to bed. "We've got a busy day tomorrow. Get some rest."

The next morning, Grandma peeked into the children's bedroom. "Good morning!" Grandma whispered.

Patrick rolled over and said, "What are we going to do today, Grandma?"

"How about a swim?" she asked.

Grace lifted her head. "I want to swim too."

"*Yeah!* I'll go get our swimsuits," Patrick said with an excited voice.

"Okay," Grandma said. "Let's have some breakfast first."

The children had a wonderful time splashing in the pool. When they were finished, they had a fun picnic on a blanket outside.

Papa looked at them with love. How grateful he was to be able to spend this time with them.

The next day, Grace and Patrick had their usual breakfast with Grandma and Papa. They loved it when Grandma would open the window blinds and start singing about how beautiful the day was going to be.

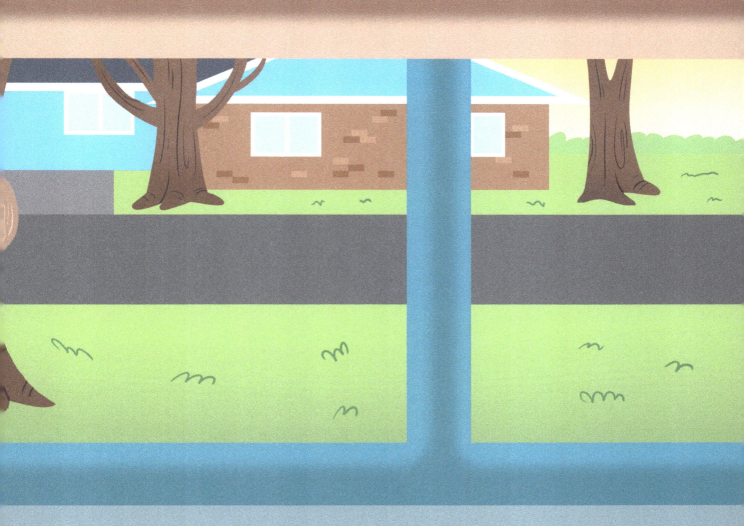

Today, they were going to the green park. They packed snacks and water and headed down the street. The park wasn't far from the house, which then made a lovely time to walk and talk along the way. Patrick and Grace were so excited that Grandma and Papa had a hard time keeping up with them.

"There it is. I can see the green tower!" said Patrick.

The children ran up to the play area. They climbed, slid down twirling slides, lay flat on the merry-go-round, and looked up to the sky.

"Wow, what a time to be grateful," Papa said to the children. Grace and Patrick agreed.

When they returned home, it was bedtime. They lay in bed and Papa read them a story. Papa kissed them good night, and Grandma hugged them and thought what a special time they had at the park.

22

The next day, the last day of the sleepover, Patrick woke up and ran into the kitchen. He knew Papa was cooking breakfast.

"Yummy!" Patrick said. It was blueberry muffins. "Can I help?"

Shortly after that, Grace wandered in to the kitchen. "Grandma, do you have any mangoes?"

"Of course I do, sweetheart," Grandma said. "Have a seat and we'll eat breakfast.

You know today is the last day of our sleepover weekend."
Patrick lowered his head and frowned.

"Now, Patrick, don't be sad. Think of what a good time we've had. Instead of being sad, maybe think about how grateful we all are for this time together," Grandma said. "You know, some children don't get to see their grandparents as much as you do."

Patrick and Grace were headed home with mom. Grace told Mom what a good time they had and wanted to know when the next sleepover was.

Patrick looked at Grace and said, "Remember what Grandma said, Grace—'Be grateful.' We'll see them soon."

Mom looked in the rearview mirror and smiled gratefully.

About the Author

Eileen Teel lives in Colorado. What brings her joy in her life is her wonderful family - husband Brian, three grown children and now grandchildren! Her Irish upbringing means she has always loved stories. After retiring from Higher Education, she began spending her time with the more important things in life-enjoying time with the grandchildren!

Be Grateful is the second book in her series, following *Be Kind*. Eileen is excited to share this new book and hopes it will bring words of a positive nature to her audience.

Enjoy this book and try to spread the message of gratitude to all that will lend an ear.

Printed in the USA
CPSIA information can be obtained
at www.ICGtesting.com
CBHW041546241024
16328CB00057B/974